HOLT

United States History

Beginnings to 1877

Tennessee

HOLT, RINEHART AND WINSTON

A Harcourt Education Company

Orlando • Austin • New York • San Diego • London

ISBN-13 978-0-03-099519-4
ISBN 0-03-099519-1

8 9 1409 11
4500318843

Contents

The Tennessee Social Studies Curriculum Standards include Content Standards and Student Performance Indicators for Eighth Grade United States History. To help you assess at which level a student is performing, Holt Social Studies has created the *TCAP Test Prep Workbook.* Designed to be used in conjunction with *Holt's United States History, Beginnings to 1877,* Tennessee Edition, this component includes the following:

Correlations: A section aligning the Tennessee Content Standards, Learning Expectations, and Student Performance Indicators to material tested in this workbook and to chapters in the Student Edition.

Tests: Test questions modeled after the TCAP test in style and content organized by Student Performance Indicators.

Answer Key: Answers to the questions are included in the *Tennessee Holt Social Studies Middle School Answer Keys.*

Tennessee United States History Performance Indicators

COURSE DESCRIPTION

[In United States History, students study the history of the United States Reconstruction to the present. The six social studies standards of essential content knowledge and four process skills are integrated for instructional purposes. Students will utilize different methods that historians use to interpret the past, including points of view and historical context.]

Learning Expectation or Performance Indicator	Page(s) in This Workbook	Chapter(s) in Student Edition
Content Standard 1.0: Culture	**1–13**	**1–17**
Culture encompasses similarities and differences among people, including their beliefs, knowledge, changes, values, and traditions. Students will explore these elements of society to develop an appreciation and respect for the variety of human cultures.		
Learning Expectations:		
1.01 Understand the nature and complexity of culture.	1–13	Prologue, 1–17
1.02 Discuss the development of major religions.	1–13	1–3
1.03 Identify the role those diverse cultures had on the development of the Americas.	1–13	Prologue, 1–17
1.04 Describe the influence of science and technology on the development of culture through time.	1–13	1–2, 12
Performance Indicators: *At Level 1, the student is able to* **8.1.spi.1.** recognize the definition of religion.	1–2	1
8.1.spi.2. identify cultures that contributed to the development of the United States (i.e., Native American, African, British, Scottish, Irish, German).	3–4	Prologue, 1–3
8.1.spi.3. recognize the influence of science and technology on the development of early American colonial cultures (i.e., compass, shipbuilding, food storage, printing press, financial markets, weaponry, transportation).	5–6	1–3
At Level 2, the student is able to **8.1.spi.4.** compare and contrast the tenets of America's early major religions (i.e., Olmec beliefs, Native American Earth/Mother spirit, African Traditional Religion, Puritanism, Quakerism).	7–8	1–3

Learning Expectation or Performance Indicator	Page(s) in This Workbook	Chapter(s) in Student Edition
8.1.spi.5. identify how religion contributed to early American society (i.e., impact on government, education, social norms, slavery, tolerance).	9–10	1–3
8.1.spi.6. interpret a time line of technological innovations.	11	12
At Level 3, the student is able to **8.1.spi.7.** recognize how immigration and cultural diffusion have influenced the character of a place (i.e., religion within certain colonies, African songs in the American South, British vs. French influences).	12–13	1–3
Content Standard 2.0: Economics	**14–33**	**12–13**
Globalization of the economy, the explosion of population growth, technological changes, and international competition compel students to understand both personally and globally production, distribution, and consumption of goods and services. Students will examine and analyze economic concepts such as basic needs versus wants, using versus saving money, and policy making versus decision making.		
Learning Expectations: **2.1** Understand fundamental economic concepts and their application to a variety of economic systems.	14–33	1–3, 12–13
2.2 Understand global economic connections, conflicts, and interdependence.	14–33	1–3
2.3 Understand the potential costs and benefits of individual economic choices in the market economy.	14–33	1–
2.4 Understand the interactions of individuals, businesses, and the government in a market economy.	14–33	10
Performance Indicators: *At Level 1, the student is able to* **8.2.spi.1.** recognize America's natural resources (i.e., land, timber, fish, animal pelts, peppers, sweet potatoes, squash, pumpkins, turkeys, peanuts, potatoes, tomatoes, tobacco, cacao, beans, and vanilla).	14–15	2
8.2.spi.2. interpret a diagram showing the steps of changing a resource into a product.	16–17	10

Learning Expectation or Performance Indicator	Page(s) in This Workbook	Chapter(s) in Student Edition
8.2.spi.3. differentiate between credit and debt.	18–19	Prologue
At Level 2, the student is able to **8.2.spi.4.** recognize the economic activities of early America (i.e., agriculture, industry, and service).	20–21	1–17
8.2.spi.5. identify various forms of taxation (i.e., tariffs, sales tax, excise tax).	22–23	Prologue, 3
8.2.spi.6. interpret a variety of economic graphs and charts with topics (i.e., the Columbian Exchange, numbers of slaves, population of colonies, population diversity).	24–25	1–17
8.2.spi.7. differentiate between a commercial and subsistence economy.	26–27	1–3
8.2.spi.8. recognize the factors that led to urbanization and industrialization in early America (i.e., religious freedom, landownership, thriving market).	28–29	1–3
At Level 3, the student is able to **8.2.spi.9.** analyze in economic terms (i.e., climate, triangle trade, infrastructure, topography) why slavery flourished in the South as opposed to the North.	30–31	12–13
8.2.spi.10. distinguish among various economic markets found in early America (i.e., traditional, monopoly, oligopoly, free competition).	32–33	1–3
Content Standard 3.0: Geography	**34–46**	**1–17**
Geography enables the students to see, understand, and appreciate the web of relationships between people, places, and environments. Students will use the knowledge, skills, and understanding of concepts within the six essential elements of geography: world in spatial terms, places and regions, physical systems, human systems, environment and society, and the uses of geography.		
Learning Expectations: **3.01** Understand how to use maps, globes, and other geographic representations, tools, and technologies to acquire, process, and report information from a spatial perspective.	34–46	1–17

Learning Expectation or Performance Indicator	Page(s) in This Workbook	Chapter(s) in Student Edition
3.02 Know the location of places and geographic features, both physical and human, in Tennessee and in the United States.	34–46	1–17
3.03 Recognize the interaction between human and physical systems.	34–46	1–17
3.04 Understand the geographic factors that determined the locations of and patterns of settlements in the United States and Tennessee.	34–46	1–3
3.05 Understand the impact of immigration and migration on a society.	34–46	14
Performance Indicators: *At Level 1, the student is able to* **8.3.spi.1.** recognize the causes and examples of migration and immigration in early America (i.e., land, religion, money, pioneer spirit, indentured servitude, displacement, and slavery).	34–35	1–3
8.3.spi.2. identify and use the key geographic elements on maps (i.e., island, floodplain, swamp, delta, marsh, harbor, cape, sea level, bay, prairie, desert, oasis, mesa, mountain, valley, glacier, canyon, cliff, plateau).	36–37	Geographic Dictionary
At Level 2, the student is able to **8.3.spi.3.** interpret examples which illustrate how cultures adapt to or change the environment (i.e., deforestation, subsistence farming, cash crop, dam and road building).	38–39	3, 12–14
8.3.spi.4. use various geographic data from maps and globes to determine longitude, latitude, distance, direction.	40	1–17
8.3.spi.5. interpret a geographic map of the early United States.	41–42	3–5
8.3.spi.6. recognize how topographical features such as mountain and river systems influenced the settlement and expansion of the United States (i.e., Cumberland Gap, Wilderness Road, Ohio and Tennessee river systems).	43–44	Prologue, 10–11
At Level 3, the student is able to **8.3.spi.7.** interpret a chart or map of population characteristics of the early United States (i.e., density, distribution, regional growth).	45–46	5, 7

Learning Expectation or Performance Indicator	Page(s) in This Workbook	Chapter(s) in Student Edition
Content Standard 4.0: Governance and Civics	**47–64**	**6**
Governance establishes structures of power and authority in order to provide order and stability. Civic efficacy requires understanding rights and responsibilities, ethical behavior, and the role of citizens within their community, nation, and world.		
Learning Expectations: **4.01** Appreciate the development of people's need to organize themselves into a system of governance.	47–64	1–6
4.02 Recognize the purposes and structure of governments.	47–64	1, 6
4.03 Understand the relationship between a place's physical, political, and cultural characteristics and the type of government that emerges from that relationship.	47–64	1–3
4.04 Discuss how cooperation and conflict among people influence the division and control resources, rights, and privileges.	47–64	1–17
4.05 Understand the rights, responsibilities, and privileges of citizens living in a democratic society.	47–64	6
4.06 Understand the role the Constitution of the United States plays in the lives of Americans.	47–64	6
4.07 Understand the role that Tennessee's government plays in Tennesseans' lives.	47–64	Tennessee State Facts
Performance Indicators: *At Level 1, the student is able to* **8.4.spi.1.** identify the rights, responsibilities, and privileges of a member of the United States of America (i.e., Declaration of Independence, Articles of Confederation, Constitution, Bill of Rights).	47–48	5–6
At Level 2, the student is able to **8.4.spi.2.** identify the purposes and structures of various systems of governance (i.e., Federalism, Confederation, Republic, Democracy, Executive, Legislative, Judicial).	49–50	6
8.4.spi.3. recognize the purpose of government and how its powers are acquired, used, and justified.	51–52	5–17
8.4.spi.4. recognize the rights and responsibilities of individuals throughout the development of the United States.	53–54	1–17

Learning Expectation or Performance Indicator	Page(s) in This Workbook	Chapter(s) in Student Edition
8.4.spi.5. identify how conditions, actions, and motivations contributed to conflict and cooperation between states, regions, and nations.	55–56	1–17
8.4.spi.6. recognize the rights guaranteed in the Bill of Rights.	57–58	6
8.4.spi.7. recognize the impact of major court decisions have had on American life, (i.e., *Marbury* v. *Madison*, *McCulloch* v. *Maryland*, *Dred Scott* v. *Sandford*).	59–60	7–8, 15
At Level 3, the student is able to **8.4.spi.8.** recognize how a right must be interpreted to balance individual rights with the need for order (i.e., freedom of speech, freedom of religion, trial by jury).	61–62	6
8.4.spi.9. analyze the contributions of Tennessee political leaders on the national scene (e.g., Andrew Jackson, Andrew Johnson, James K. Polk, Sequoyah, Sam Houston).	63–64	8–11, 17
Content Standard 5.0: History	**65–105**	**1–17**
History involves people, events, and issues. Students will evaluate evidence to develop comparative and casual analyses and to interpret primary sources. They will construct sound historical arguments and perspectives on which informed decisions in contemporary life can be based.		
Learning Expectations: **Era 1—Three Worlds Meet (Beginnings to 1620)** **5.01** Identify ancient civilizations of the Americas.	65–105	1
5.02 Understand the place of historical events in the context of past, present and future.	65–105	1–2
5.03 Use historical information acquired from a variety of sources to develop critical sensitivities such as skepticism regarding attitudes, values, and behaviors of people in different historical contexts.	65–105	1–2
5.04 Recognize Tennessee's role within the early development of the Americas.	65–105	Prologue
Era 2—Colonization and Settlement (1585–1763) **5.05** Identify the role desire for freedom played in the settlement of the New World.	65–105	2–3

Learning Expectation or Performance Indicator	Page(s) in This Workbook	Chapter(s) in Student Edition
5.06 Understand the place of historical events in the context of past, present, and future.	65–105	2–3
5.07 Use historical information acquired from a variety of sources to develop critical sensitivities such as skepticism regarding attitudes, values, and behaviors of people in different historical contexts.	65–105	2–3
5.08 Understand the social, cultural, and political events that shaped African slavery in colonial America.	65–105	2–3
5.09 Recognize Tennessee's role within colonial America.	65–105	Prologue, 2–3
Era 3—Revolution and the New Nation (1754–1820) **5.10** Understand the causes and results of the American Revolution.	65–105	3–5
5.11 Understand the place of historical events in the context of past, present, and future.	65–105	3–5
5.12 Demonstrate how to use historical information acquired from a variety of sources to develop critical sensitivities such as skepticism regarding attitudes, values, and behaviors of people in different historical contexts.	65–105	3–5
5.13 Identify Tennessee's role within early development of the nation.	65–105	Prologue, 3–5
Era 4—Expansion and Reform (1801–1861) **5.14** Identify American territorial expansion efforts and its effects on relations with European powers and Native Americans.	65–105	5, 7–15
5.15 Discuss sectional differences brought on by the western movement, expansion of slavery, and emerging industrialization.	65–105	5, 7–15
5.16 Recognize successes and failures of reform movements of the early 1800s to develop critical sensitivities such as skepticism regarding attitudes, values, and behaviors of people in different historical contexts.	65–105	5, 7–15
5.17 Identify Tennessee's role within expansion of the nation.	65–105	Prologue, 5, 7–15

Learning Expectation or Performance Indicator	Page(s) in This Workbook	Chapter(s) in Student Edition
Era 5—Civil War and Reconstruction (1850–1877) **5.18** Recognize the causes, course, and consequences of the Civil War.	65–105	16–17
5.19 Identify the contributions of African Americans from slavery to Reconstruction.	65–105	1–17
5.20 Identify Tennessee's role within the Civil War.	65–105	Prologue, 16–17
Performance Indicators: *At Level 1, the student is able to* **8.5.spi.1.** contrast the characteristics of major native civilizations of the Americas.	65–67	1
8.5.spi.2. read a time line and order events of the past.	68–70	1–17
8.5.spi.3. differentiate between a primary and secondary source.	71–73	15
8.5.spi.4. recognize causes and consequences of conflict (i.e., French and Indian War, Revolutionary War, War of 1812).	74–76	1–17
At Level 2, the student is able to **8.5.spi.5.** recognize consequences of the westward expansion of the United States.	77–79	11, 14–17
8.5.spi.6. classify the characteristics of major historic events into causes and effects (i.e., exploration, colonization, revolution, expansion, and Civil War).	80–82	1–17
8.5.spi.7. recognize the historical impacts of European settlement in North America.	83–85	1–4
8.5.spi.8. determine the social, political, and economic factors that contributed to the institution of slavery in America.	86–88	1–3, 13
8.5.spi.9. interpret a time line, detailing the development of political parties in the United States to the Civil War.	89–91	15
8.5.spi.10. interpret maps, time lines, and charts that illustrate key elements of history (i.e., expansion, economics, politics, society).	92–94	1–17
At Level 3, the student is able to **8.5.spi.11.** identify conclusions about historical events using primary and secondary sources.	95–97	1–17

Learning Expectation or Performance Indicator	Page(s) in This Workbook	Chapter(s) in Student Edition
8.5.spi.12. differentiate between primary and secondary source documents.	98–100	15
8.5.spi.13. examine the demographic changes brought about by westward movement (i.e., slavery, industrialization, and Native American relocation).	101–102	11–16
8.5.spi.14. recognize the course of conflicts, including major battles, alliances, strategy, leadership, resources, or technology, using a diagram for the Revolutionary War.	103–105	4
Content Standard 6.0: Individuals, Groups, and Interactions	**106–117**	**1–17**
Personal development and identity are shaped by factors including culture, groups, and institutions. Central to this development are exploration, identification, and analysis of how individuals and groups work independently and cooperatively.		
Learning Expectations: **6.01** Recognize the impact of individual and group decisions on citizens and communities.	106–117	1–17
6.02 Understand how groups can impact change at the local, state, national, and world levels.	106–117	6
Performance Indicators: *At Level 1, the student is wable to* **8.6.spi.1.** identify the impact of individual and group decisions on historical events.	106–107	1–17
8.6.spi.2. recognize the impact groups have on change at the local, state, national, and world levels.	108–109	1–17
At Level 2, the student is able to **8.6.spi.3.** recognize examples of stereotyping, prejudice, conformity, and altruism in early American history.	110–111	1–3
8.6.spi.4. identify the role of institutions in furthering both continuity and change (i.e., governments, churches, families, schools, communities).	112–113	3, 6, 14
8.6.spi.5. recognize how groups and institutions work together to meet common needs.	114–115	6
At Level 3, the student is able to **8.6.spi.6.** debate the effectiveness of a public policy or citizen behavior in realizing the ideals of a democracy.	116–117	6

1. Master the question

Have you ever said, "I knew the answer, but I thought the question asked something else"? Be very sure that you know what a question is asking. Read the question at least twice before reading the answer choices. Approach it as you would a mystery story or a riddle. Look for clues. Watch especially for words like *not* and *except*—they tell you to look for the choice that is false or different from the other choices or opposite in some way.

2. Track your time

Use all the time you are given to take a test in order to avoid making errors. Here are some checkpoints to help you monitor your time.

- How many questions should be completed when one-quarter of the time is gone? when half the time is gone?

- What should the clock read when you are halfway through the questions?

- If you find yourself behind your checkpoints, you can speed up.

- If you are ahead, you can—and should—slow down.

3. Study the directions

In order to follow the directions you have to know what the directions are! Read through the directions once. Then read the directions again. Study the answer sheet. How is it laid out? What about the answer choices? How are they arranged?

A   B
C   D   or   A   B   C   D

Be very sure you know exactly what to do and how to do it before you make your first mark.

4. Take it all in

When you finally hear the words "You may begin," briefly preview the test to get a mental map of your tasks.

- Know how many questions you have to complete.

- Know where to stop.

- Set your time checkpoints.

- Do the easy sections first; easy questions can be worth just as many points as hard ones.

5. Negatives do not fit

Be sure to watch for negative words in the questions, such as *never*, *unless*, *not*, and *except*. When a question contains one of these negative words, look for the answer that does not fit with the other answers.

6. Jot it down quick

You might have made a special effort to memorize some information for the test. If you are worried you will forget it as soon as the testing period begins, jot it down on the back of your test or on your scratch paper as soon as the teacher begins the test. Then go on and work on the test itself.

7. Anticipate the answers

Before you read the answer choices, answer the question yourself. Then read the choices. If the answer you gave is among the choices listed, it is probably correct.

8. Go with your instinct

Your first impulse is most often correct. Be careful about changing your answers on multiple-choice or true-false questions. If you do decide to change your answer, be totally confident in making the change.

9. Spot those numbers

Have you ever said, "I got off by one and spent all my time trying to fix my answer sheet"? Make it a habit to

- match the number of each question to the numbered space on the answer sheet every time

- leave the answer blank if you skip a question

- keep a list of your blank spaces on scratch paper or somewhere else— but not on your answer sheet; the less you have to erase, the better

10. I'm done!

When you think you are finished with your test, you still need to check it. First, take a look at the clock and see how much time you have left. Go back and review your answers for any careless mistakes you may have made, such as leaving a question blank or putting two answers to one question. Be sure to erase any stray marks, review the hardest questions you answered, and turn the test in at the end of the time period. You gain nothing from finishing first—or last, for that matter.

Culture   United States History

1   **Which of the following statements *best* defines the term *religion*?**

   A   the belief in a single Supreme Being

   B   the use of logic to pursue knowledge

   C   beliefs and practices associated with worship

   D   the art of guiding or controlling a government

> **polytheism:** the belief that there is more than one god or spirit

2   **Based on the definition above, polytheism is a part of which of the following religious traditions?**

   F   the Aztec religious tradition

   G   Protestants

   H   Jews

   J   Muslims

Culture

United States History

3   Which religious tradition regards the pope as the absolute leader of the church?

 A Anglicanism

 (B) Catholicism

 C Puritanism

 D Judaism

4   Which of the following colonies allowed only church members to vote in public elections when it was founded?

 F New Amsterdam

 (G) the Massachusetts Bay Colony

 H Virginia

 J North Carolina

Culture

United States History

Dominant Language Families

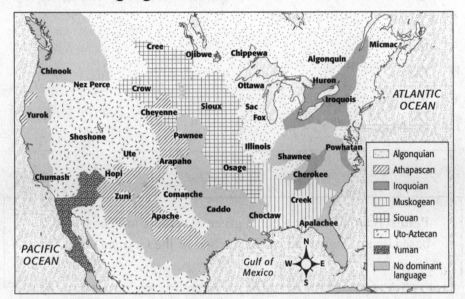

5   **Based on the map above, where were the Huron and Iroquois groups located?**

    A   the Northwest

    B   the Northeast

    C   the Southwest

    D   the Southeast

6   **Based on the map above, what were the dominant language and Native American groups of the Southwest?**

    F   Choctaw, Creek, and Apalachee

    G   Sioux, Pawnee, and Fox

    H   Apache, Hopi, and Zuni

    J   Chinook and Nez Perce

7   **Immigrants to the United States from which of the following countries were predominantly Catholic?**

A   Italy

B   Russia

C   England

D   the Netherlands

> **Pennsylvania Dutch:** a name given to settlers in Pennsylvania based on an English mispronunciation of the German word *Deutsch*.

8   **What nation were the so-called Pennsylvania Dutch actually from?**

F   England

G   Germany

H   the Netherlands

J   Ireland

9 **Which of the following inventions gave European colonists the greatest military advantage when fighting Native Americans?**

A   suits of steel armor

B   gunpowder and firearms

C   naval sailing ships

D   hot-air balloons

The first turnpike in the colonies went into use in 1794.

10 **Which of the following _best_ defines the term _turnpike_?**

F   part of a printing press

G   a weapon mounted on a wagon

H   the axle of a waterwheel for a factory

J   a private toll road

11   Colonists who wanted to travel a long distance quickly were most likely to use which of the following transportation methods?

A   riding a train

B   walking

C   going by steamboat

D   sailing in a sailboat

12   In 1793 Samuel Slater opened the first of what in the United States?

F   bank

G   factory for interchangeable parts

H   public road

J   textile mill

> "We shall be as a city upon a Hill, the eyes of all people are upon us."
>
> —John Winthrop

13 **John Winthrop was a leader of what religious group, whose members helped found the English colonies?**

A   Catholics

B   Baptists

C   Puritans

D   African traditional religions

---

shamanism: a belief system in which wise and powerful individuals known as shamans communicate with spirits of nature and ancestors on behalf of their people

14 **Which of the following cultural groups often practiced some form of shamanism?**

F   Quakers

G   Native Americans

H   French Huguenots

J   Protestants

15 **Leaders of which society developed an extremely complex calendar, in part to help them carry out religious rituals?**

A   the Iroqouis

B   the New England colonies

C   the Mississippians

D   the Mayas

16 **Which of the following faiths expressed a strong belief in nonviolence as one of its core principles?**

F   the Aztec religion

G   the faith of Native American peoples such as the Comanches

H   Quakerism

J   Catholicism

Culture

United States History

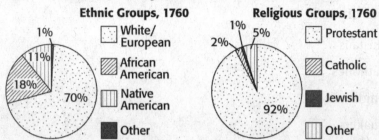

America's Population, 1760: 1.8 million

Ethnic Groups, 1760

- 1%
- 11%
- 18%
- 70%

White/European
African American
Native American
Other

Religious Groups, 1760

- 1%
- 2%
- 5%
- 92%

Protestant
Catholic
Jewish
Other

17 Based on the information in the graphs above, which religious group had the greatest influence on colonial society?

A   Catholics

B   Jews

C   Protestants

D   Other

18 Which two colonies were founded on principles of religious tolerance and permitted public worship for both Catholics and Jews?

F   Massachusetts and Connecticut

G   North Carolina and South Carolina

H   New Jersey and Delaware

J   Pennsylvania and Rhode Island

19 The colleges Harvard and Yale were founded by members of which religious group?

    A   Puritans

    B   Catholics

    C   Anglicans

    D   Quakers

20 Which religious group was one of the first to demand that its members oppose slavery and give up their own slaves?

    F   Puritans

    G   Catholics

    H   Anglicans

    J   Quakers

Culture

United States History

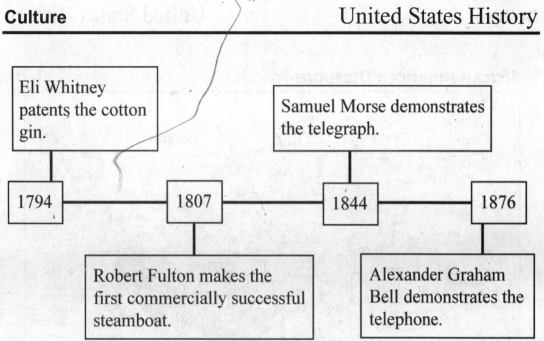

21 Based on the time line shown above, place the following inventions in the order of their invention: telegraph, cotton gin, and telephone.

   A   telegraph, telephone, cotton gin

   B   telephone, cotton gin, telegraph

   C   cotton gin, telegraph, telephone

   D   telephone, telegraph, cotton gin

---

22 If you lived in 1850, which of the inventions shown above could you have used?

   F   the cotton gin and steamboat

   G   the cotton gin, steamboat, and telegraph

   H   only the telegraph

   J   all of the inventions

African American Diaspora

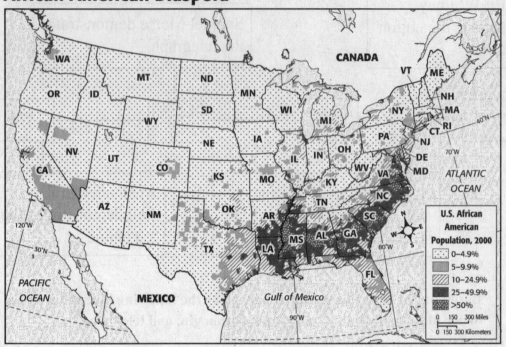

23   Based on the information in the map above, where was the greatest
      concentration of African Americans in 2000?

      A   the Northeast

      B   the South

      C   the Midwest

      D   the West

24   Identify some of the ways in which the African American influence in this
      region has affected its culture.

      F   through African-influenced musical forms, such as gospel and blues

      G   through African American cuisine

      H   culture changed little over the periods shown

      J   all of the above

25   **Which of the following states has a strong cultural influence from its French settlers?**

A   Massachusetts

B   Florida

C   New York

D   Louisiana

26   **Irish immigrants to the United States settled mainly in which of the following areas?**

F   western ranches

G   Midwestern farms

H   northern cities

J   southern plantations

Food Crops

oats, potatoes, pumpkins, rice, tomatoes, wheat

1   **Which of the crops listed above were native to the Americas?**

   A   potatoes, rice, and wheat

   B   potatoes, pumpkins, and tomatoes

   C   potatoes, oats, and wheat

   D   oats, rice, and wheat

2   **Native Americans in the southeastern region of North America relied on which three food crops?**

   F   beans, maize, and squash

   G   beans, peanuts, and potatoes

   H   acorns, barley, and rice

   J   berries, fruits, and nuts

Economics   United States History

3   **Which of the following goods did Native Americans trade with French and English colonists?**

A   gold and precious gems

B   iron ore and coal

C   silk and spices

D   animal furs and pelts

4   **Which of the following reasons for settling in the Americas was the *most* significant for early colonists?**

F   No diseases existed in the Americas.

G   Much more land was available than in Europe.

H   The American landscape was more attractive than in Europe.

J   The climate in North America was milder than in Europe.

Changing Cotton Into Clothing

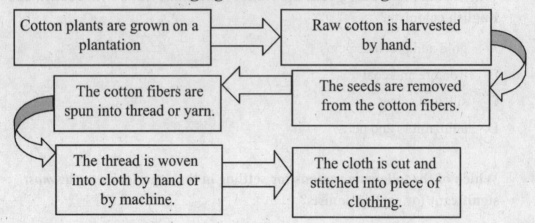

5 **Which step shown in the diagram above comes just before cotton is made into articles of clothing?**

A Cotton threads are woven into cotton cloth.

B Seeds are removed from the cotton fibers.

C Cotton fibers are spun into threads.

D Cotton fibers are dyed.

6 **Which of the steps shown in the diagram above are *most* likely to take place in a factory?**

F harvesting, spinning, and stitching

G spinning, weaving, and stitching

H removing seeds, spinning, and weaving

J growing, harvesting, and weaving

Economics   United States History

7   **Why might good transportation have been important to the production of cotton cloth?**

   A   Cotton farmers needed to travel to and from their fields.

   B   Spinners and weavers needed to travel to plantations to make cloth.

   C   Raw cotton needed to be shipped to factories to be made into cloth.

   D   Customers needed to travel to the South to buy cotton goods.

8   **Why were the seeds removed from raw cotton?**

   F   Leaving the seeds in created lumpy cloth that was not in fashion.

   G   Many people were allergic to cotton seeds.

   H   The cotton seeds were fed to the farmer's livestock.

   J   The sticky seeds kept the cotton fibers from being spun.

9   **Money, goods, and services loaned by one party to another are known as**

   A   securities

   B   stocks

   C   credit

   D   income

10   **Which of the following *best* defines the term *interest*?**

   F   an additional payment made for the use of loaned money

   G   an initial cash payment on an installment loan

   H   the change in the value of money over time

   J   a fee paid for a required license

Economics   United States History

11   What is debt?

A   an imbalance in foreign trade

B   the loss in value of a piece of property

C   a tax on imports

D   money owed by a borrower to a lender

Loan Example

> A Farmer borrows $3,000 from a Merchant to buy new
> farmland and promises to repay this amount by a certain date.

12   Based on the information above, which person is the debtor and which person is the creditor?

F   The Farmer is the creditor, and the Merchant is the debtor.

G   The Farmer is the debtor, and the Merchant is the creditor.

H   Both the Farmer and the Merchant are creditors.

J   Both the Farmer and the Merchant are debtors.

Colonial Economic Activities

> trade, shipping goods, shipbuilding, fishing

13　The list above *best* describes the economic activities of which colonial region?

A　the southern colonies

B　the New England colonies

C　the Middle colonies

D　the Caribbean colonies

> **cash crop:** an agricultural product grown primarily to be sold for profits, not for personal use

14　Which of the following cash crops was the *most* important to the southern English colonies in the 1700s?

F　cotton

G　corn

H　tobacco

J　cacao

Economics   United States History

15 **Which colonial region was the primary producer of grains such as wheat?**

A   the southern colonies

B   the New England colonies

C   the Middle colonies

D   grain production equal in all colonies

16 **Young colonists sent to learn skilled trades such as blacksmithing, printing, or weaving were known as**

F   apprentices

G   blue-collar workers

H   white-collar workers

J   interns

17 **Which of the following _best_ defines the term _tariff_?**

A   a tax on goods made without a proper license

B   a tax on goods inherited from family members

C   a tax on goods exported to other countries

D   a tax on goods imported from other countries

18 **Which of the following is _not_ a reason why a country might raise its tariff rates on certain goods?**

F   to encourage people to buy those goods

G   to discourage people from buying those goods

H   to raise money for the government

J   to protect local industries from foreign competition

> **excise tax:** a tax collected on the sale or production of certain goods, particularly luxury goods

19 Based on the information above, which of the following items would *most* likely be subject to an excise tax?

A   milk

B   jewelry

C   shoes

D   cattle

> Person A goes to the store and buys a carton of eggs priced at $1.00. When Person A pays for the eggs, the cost is $1.10.

20 Based on the above reading, what is the amount of sales tax paid by Person A?

F   1%

G   5%

H   10%

J   not an example of sales tax

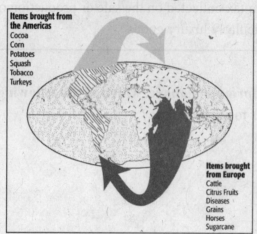

The Columbian Exchange

Items brought from
the Americas
Cocoa
Corn
Potatoes
Squash
Tobacco
Turkeys

Items brought
from Europe
Cattle
Citrus Fruits
Diseases
Grains
Horses
Sugarcane

21 **Based on the information shown in the diagram above, the Columbian Exchange is best described as**

A the movement of people between Europe and the Americas

B the name of the regions explored by Columbus

C the movement of animals and plants between Europe and the Americas

D the goods traded between Native Americans and colonists

---

22 **Which of the following statements is *best* supported by the evidence in the diagram above?**

F Native Americans did not practice agriculture before Europeans arrived.

G Crops from the Americas were less valuable than the crops from Europe.

H Crops from Europe were less valuable than crops from the Americas.

J Native Americans did not ride horses before the arrival of Europeans.

Slaves Brought to the Americas, 1493-1810

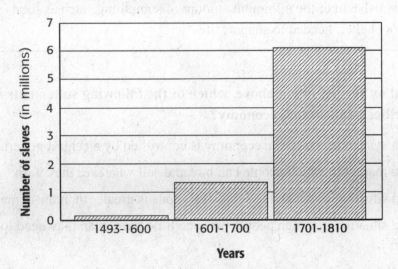

23   **Based on the information in the graph above, about how many slaves were brought to the Americas between 1601 and 1700?**

A   about 100,000

B   less than 1 million

C   slightly more than 1 million

D   nearly 2 million

24   **Based on the information in the graph above, which of the following statements *best* reflects the trend in the slave trade?**

F   It increased steadily over the years shown, peaking in 1810.

G   It began slowly and increased sharply beginning in 1701.

H   It showed little change over the periods shown.

J   It declined during the 1600s before increasing in 1701.

> **subsistence:** the minimum amount of something, such as food or shelter, needed to support life

25 **Based on the definition above, which of the following statements *best* describes a subsistence economy?**

    A   a system in which the economy is controlled by a central government

    B   a market in which people can buy and sell whatever they wish

    C   a situation in which the supply of goods is greater than the demand

    D   a situation in which people produce little more than they need to survive

26 **Which situation is *most* likely to occur in a subsistence economy?**

    F   People spend most of their energy producing goods for trade.

    G   People have few possessions and produce little surplus.

    H   People can buy only goods approved by the government.

    J   People pay high taxes on the goods that they buy.

27   Why are markets important to a commercial economy? Choose the *best* answer.

    A   The government taxes markets to raise money.

    B   There is no money, so people must trade goods at markets.

    C   People use markets to buy and sell goods and services they produce.

    D   Markets are where people grow the crops they need to survive.

28   Which of the following professional people is *least* likely to be found in a commercial economy?

    F   a hunter-gatherer

    G   a craftsperson

    H   a banker

    J   a merchant

Economics   United States History

**Urban vs. Rural
Population, 1790**

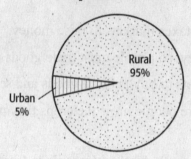

29   **Based on the graph above, which statement most accurately describes the
      population of America in 1790?**

      A   The majority of people lived in the country.

      B   The majority of people lived in cities.

      C   The population was evenly divided between city and country.

      D   Most people lived in neither the city nor the country.

30   **Which of the following factors encouraged people to move to cities in the
      colonial period?**

      F   Cities were sources of valuable natural resources.

      G   Cities were centers of trade and commerce.

      H   Cities had inexpensive land.

      J   Cities had healthier living conditions than the country.

31   **How did the growth of American industry affect the population of cities?**

A   Cities shrank as people left to work in factories in the country.

B   Cities shrank as people left because of industrial pollution.

C   Cities grew as people came looking for manufacturing jobs.

D   The growth of industry had little effect on city population.

32   **When the Industrial Revolution began in the United States, what was the specialization of most of the first factories?**

F   making guns

G   making textiles

H   making household goods

J   making steel

Economics   United States History

---

33 **Which of the following is a reason why the slave population in the southern colonies was so much higher than in the northern colonies?**

A   Slavery was illegal in the northern colonies.

B   Slaves from Africa grew sick in the climate of the North.

C   Northerners used Native American rather than African slaves.

D   The southern economy relied upon slave labor.

34 **Why were cash crops such as cotton and sugar grown in the South but not in the North?**

F   No demand existed for these crops in the North.

G   Cotton and sugar would not grow in the colder northern climate.

H   Growing cotton and sugar was less profitable than growing wheat.

J   The North did not have enough fertile land to grow cash crops.

Economics   United States History

35   **How was the spread of cotton production connected to the spread of slavery?**

   A   Cotton plantations relied heavily on slave labor.

   B   More slaves were needed to work in factories making cotton cloth.

   C   Cotton grown in America was traded for slaves from Africa.

   D   Cotton plantations required fewer slaves than tobacco plantations.

> **triangle trade:** a trade network in which goods and slaves were shipped between England, the West Indies, West Africa, and the American colonies

36   **Which of the following is *not* a way that the North profited from slave labor in the South?**

   F   Northern textile factories bought large amounts of southern cotton.

   G   Northern merchants took part in the slave trade.

   H   Northern companies built many railroads to connect southern plantations.

   J   Northern merchants profited from the triangle trade.

37   **A company is said to have a monopoly on a product when**

A   It does not have to pay taxes when exporting that product.

B   It competes with other companies to make and sell that product.

C   It is the only company that makes and sells that product.

D   It is required by law to sell the product at a fixed price.

38   **In a free market**

F   goods and services do not cost money

G   the cost of goods and services is set by supply and demand

H   the government sets the minimum cost of goods and services

J   the government sets the maximum cost of goods and services

> **mercantilism:** the practice of creating and maintaining wealth
> by carefully controlling trade

39 Based on the definition given above, which of the following is the *best* example of mercantilism?

A Colonists are encouraged to be self-sufficient.

B Colonists are told to buy goods from whoever has the best prices.

C Colonists are allowed to sell some goods only to certain countries.

D Colonists are not allowed to export any goods at all.

40 Native American groups who relied on hunting and gathering for their needs were taking part in a

F traditional economy

G command economy

H mixed economy

J socialist economy

1   **Why did the Puritans found a colony in North America?**

   A   They hoped to find gold and silver.

   B   They were searching for the Northwest Passage.

   C   They were seeking religious freedom.

   D   They were declaring independence from England.

2   **In exchange for paid passage to the colonies, an indentured servant promised to**

   F   serve in the British army for a set number of years

   G   work for his or her master for a set number of years

   H   convert Native Americans to Christianity

   J   build forts along the frontier

> **pioneers:** people who are the first to settle in a region

3 **Which of the following attracted pioneers to the early American frontier?**

A   friendly relations with Native Americans

B   the availability of land

C   the desire to escape fighting on the east coast

D   rewards offered by the English Crown

---

4 **Why did Thomas Hooker leave the Massachusetts Bay Colony to found his own settlement?**

F   He wanted to found a more democratic colony.

G   He wanted to sign a new treaty with local Native Americans.

H   He wanted to found a Catholic colony.

J   He wanted to found a colony where slavery was illegal.

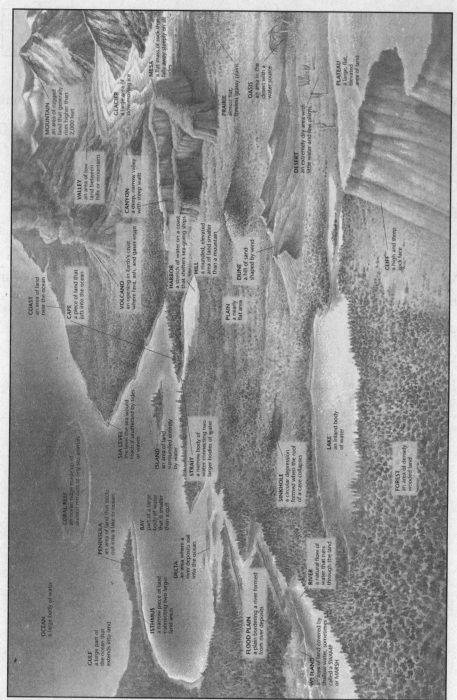

5   **Based on the information in the diagram above, where would you find an oasis?**

A   in an area of land covered by shallow water

B   along the coastline

C   in an area surrounded by desert

D   in a forested area

6 **Based on the diagram on the facing page, what is the difference between a plateau and a hill?**

   F   A hill is elevated, whereas a plateau is not.

   G   A hill is rounded on top, whereas a plateau is flat.

   H   A hill is larger than a plateau.

   J   Hills are found near the coast, whereas plateaus are not.

7 **Based on the diagram on the facing page, how are a flood plain and a delta similar?**

   A   Both are formed by soil deposited by a river.

   B   Both are depressions formed by collapsing caves.

   C   Both are found mainly in desert areas.

   D   Both are types of land that stick out into an ocean.

8 **Which of the following geographic features is *not* a body of water?**

   F   strait

   G   harbor

   H   cape

   J   bay

Railroad Resources

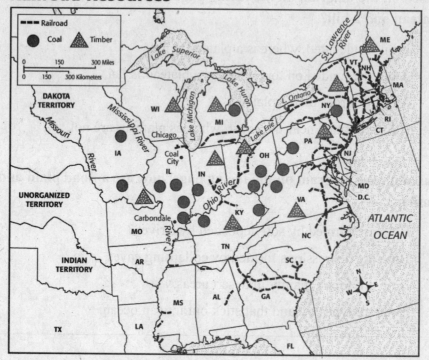

9 Based on the map shown above, where was the greatest concentration of railroads in the United States?

A   the South

B   the West

C   the Northeast

D   the Midwest

10 What is one way in which Americans changed the environment that is *not* shown in the map above?

F   digging coal mines

G   chopping down trees for wood

H   building railroads

J   digging canals

Geography   **United States History**

11   **Which of the following cash crops did southern farmers introduce to the Americas?**

     A   indigo

     B   tobacco

     C   squash

     D   maize

12   **How did the Pueblo peoples in the Southwest adapt to their harsh living conditions?**

     F   They hunted the roaming herds of buffalo.

     G   They fished and gathered wild mushrooms.

     H   They built large irrigation systems for their crops.

     J   They gathered wild acorns.

Geography

United States History

North America after the Treaty of Paris of 1783

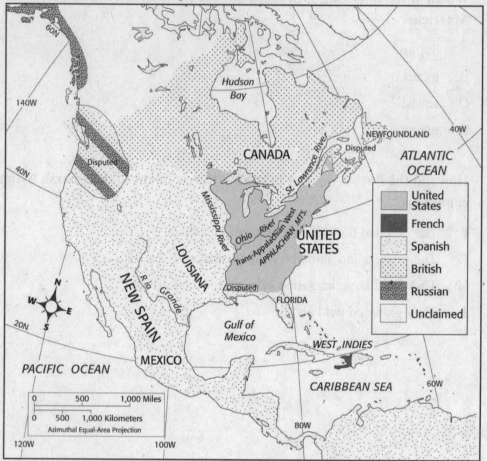

13 Based on the map above, France's possessions in the Americas lay between which lines of longitude?

    A   120° W and 100° W

    B   100° W and 80° W

    C   80° W and 60° W

    D   60° W and 40° W

14 Which country controlled the territory located at 40° N 80° W?

    F   Britain

    G   United States

    H   Spain

    J   Russia

Geography

United States History

Land Ordinance of 1785

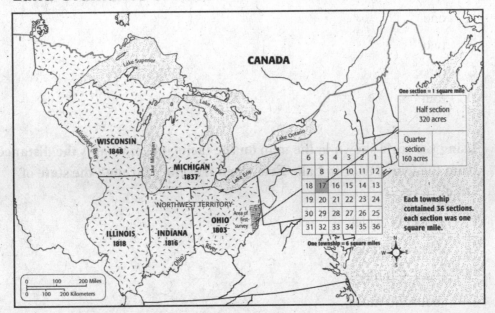

15 On the map above, which geographic feature forms the western border of Wisconsin and Illinois?

A   the Ohio River

B   the Mississippi River

C   Lake Michigan

D   Lake Huron

16 Based on the information in the map above, how many acres were in a section?

F   36

G   160

H   320

J   640

Geography   United States History

17 How many of the Great Lakes border the state of Michigan?

   A   one

   B   two

   C   three

   D   four

18 Using the scale shown in the map on the facing page, what is the distance from the Ohio River to Lake Erie when traveling through the state of Ohio?

   F   about 100 miles

   G   about 200 miles

   H   about 400 miles

   J   about 500 miles

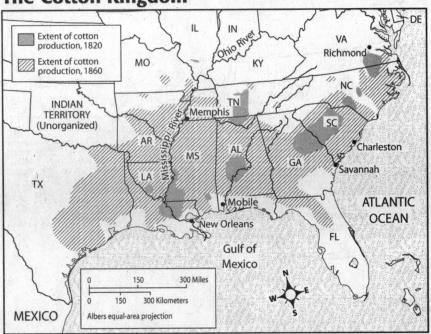

The Cotton Kingdom

19   How did the presence of major rivers influence the spread of cotton
     growing shown in the map above?

     A   Cotton grows only alongside riverbanks.

     B   Rivers provided a way to transport cotton to market.

     C   Rivers supplied all the water needed to grow the cotton.

     D   Rivers provided power for farm machinery.

20   Around which geographic feature shown in the map above was cotton
     growing *least* common?

     F   the Gulf of Mexico

     G   the Mississippi River

     H   the Appalachian Mountains

     J   the Atlantic Ocean

Choosing Sides

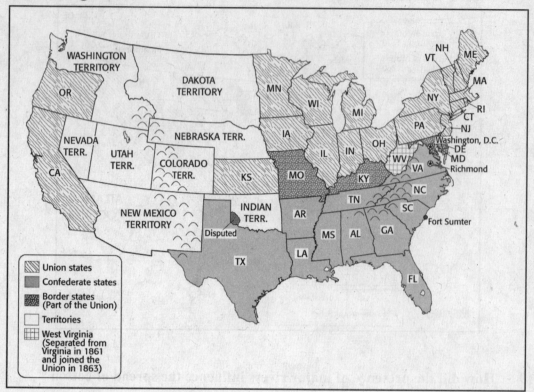

21 **Looking at the map above, which geographic feature is more common in the far western United States than in the East?**

A   large lakes

B   mountain ranges

C   major river systems

D   flat plains

22 **How might the topography shown on this map have affected the settlement of the West?**

F   It would have made farming in the West easier.

G   It would have made the West look familiar to settlers from the East.

H   It would have made it easier for settlers to travel west.

J   It would have made it harder for settlers to travel west.

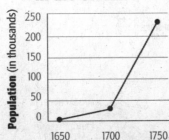

**Slave Populations
In the Colonies**

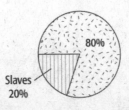

**Total Population,
1750**

23 Based on the information in the graphs above, which of the following statements *best* describes how the slave population in the colonies changed from 1700 to 1750?

A   It grew 10 times larger.

B   It doubled in size.

C   It grew by about 200,000.

D   It grew by about 250,000.

24 Based on the information in the graphs above, how did the number of nonslaves compare to the number of slaves in the colonies in 1750?

F   There were three times as many nonslaves as slaves.

G   There were four times as many nonslaves as slaves.

H   There were about 20,000 slaves and 80,000 nonslaves.

J   The population of nonslaves grew by 80 percent, and the population of slaves, by 20 percent.

Ratification of the Federal Constitution, 1787-1790

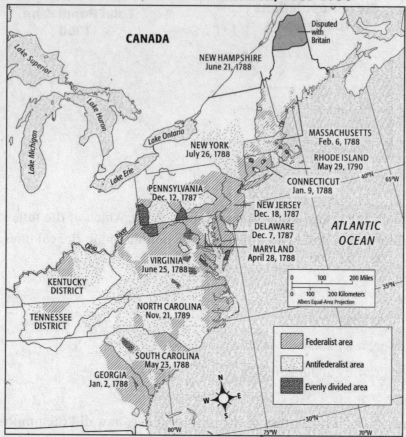

CANADA

NEW HAMPSHIRE
June 21, 1788

Disputed with Britain

MASSACHUSETTS
Feb. 6, 1788

NEW YORK
July 26, 1788

RHODE ISLAND
May 29, 1790

CONNECTICUT
Jan. 9, 1788

PENNSYLVANIA
Dec. 12, 1787

NEW JERSEY
Dec. 18, 1787

DELAWARE
Dec. 7, 1787

MARYLAND
April 28, 1788

VIRGINIA
June 25, 1788

ATLANTIC
OCEAN

KENTUCKY
DISTRICT

TENNESSEE
DISTRICT

NORTH CAROLINA
Nov. 21, 1789

SOUTH CAROLINA
May 23, 1788

GEORGIA
Jan. 2, 1788

Lake Superior · Lake Huron · Lake Michigan · Lake Ontario · Lake Erie · Ohio River

0   100   200 Miles
0   100   200 Kilometers
Albers Equal-Area Projection

Federalist area
Antifederalist area
Evenly divided area

25   **Based on the information in the map above, which of the following states were entirely Federalist?**

A   New York

B   Massachusetts

C   Delaware

D   Connecticut

26   **Which of the following states was split between Federalist, Antifederalist, and evenly divided regions?**

F   New Jersey

G   Pennsylvania

H   New York

J   Rhode Island

Governance and Civics   United States History

> **unalienable:** incapable of being given away, surrendered, or transferred

1   **What rights does the Declaration of Independence refer to as *unalienable* rights?**

   A   life, liberty, and the protection of property

   B   liberty, equality, and prosperity

   C   life, liberty, and the pursuit of happiness

   D   freedom of speech and religion

2   **Which of the following are U.S. citizens *not* required to do by law?**

   F   report to serve on public juries if called

   G   vote in all public elections

   H   pay taxes levied by the state and federal governments

   J   appear in court to testify if summoned

> "Nor shall any State deprive any person of life, liberty, or property, without due process of law; nor deny to any person within its jurisdiction the equal protection of the laws."
>
> —Fourteenth Amendment to the U.S. Constitution

3   **Due process of law is *best* described as**

A   a formal request to take away someone's property

B   the required waiting period before someone can be tried in court

C   a trial by jury

D   the fair application of the law to a person's case

---

4   **Which of the following is a requirement for U.S. citizens to vote in a public election?**

F   They must be at least 18 years of age.

G   They must be at least 19 years of age.

H   They must be at least 20 years of age.

J   They must be at least 21 years of age.

5   **A republic is a form of government *best* described as**

     A   one in which the people rule themselves

     B   one in which the people elect representatives to rule for them

     C   one in which all power is in the hands of a single person

     D   one in which all citizens meet regularly to discuss issues

---

> "The Congress shall have Power . . . To declare war . . ."
>
>   —Article I, Section 8, of the U.S. Constitution
>
>
> "The President shall be Commander in Chief of the Army and Navy of the United States . . ."
>
>   —Article 2, Section 2, of the U.S. Constitution

6   **Based on the information shown above, which of the following statements is *most* accurate?**

     F   Declaring and fighting a war require the cooperation of the Congress and the president.

     G   The president can order U.S. forces to go to war whenever necessary.

     H   Congress controls the military during peacetime, whereas the president controls the military during wartime.

     J   Congress directs the actions of the military during times of war.

7 **The legislative branch of the United States includes**

A the Supreme Court and the federal court system

B the Senate and the House of Representatives

C the Department of Defense and the Department of Justice

D the president and vice president

8 **Which of the following terms describes a system of government in which power is divided between a national government and several state governments?**

F confederation

G executive

H unitary system

J federalism

> "That to secure these rights, Governments are instituted among Men, deriving their just powers from the consent of the governed. That whenever any Form of Government becomes destructive of these ends, it is the Right of the People to alter or abolish it, and to institute new government . . ."
>
> —Declaration of Independence

9   **Based on the information shown above, what did the signers of the Declaration of Independence believe was the *main* purpose of government?**

     A   to protect the rights of its citizens

     B   to destroy rival governments

     C   to create new institutions

     D   to pass laws and regulations

10   **According to the quotation shown above, from where does a just government gain its authority?**

     F   the divine right of kings

     G   the act of revolution

     H   the approval of its own people

     J   the approval of its elected officials

11   **Under the Constitution, the state governments have the power to**

    A   regulate trade between the states

    B   coin and print their own money

    C   tax their own citizens

    D   enter treaties with foreign governments

12   **Who must vote to approve amendments to the Constitution before they are ratified?**

    F   legislatures or conventions in two-thirds of the states

    G   legislatures or conventions in three-fourths of the states

    H   three-fourths of the citizens voting in a national referendum

    J   a simple majority of both houses of Congress

> "Neither slavery nor involuntary servitude, except as a
> punishment for a crime whereof the party shall have been duly
> convicted, shall exist within the United States, or any place
> subject to their jurisdiction."
>
> —Thirteenth Amendment to the U.S. Constitution

**13   The Thirteenth Amendment was passed during what period in U.S.
history?**

A   the American Revolution

B   the ratification of the U.S. Constitution

C   the Civil War

D   the Progressive Era

14   What is the purpose of draft laws?

F   They require all eligible men to serve in the military.

G   They require all veterans to return to active-duty status.

H   They require all U.S. citizens to house members of the military.

J   They replace civilian courts with military courts during wartime.

15   Which amendment gave women in the United States the right to vote?

A   the Fifteenth Amendment

B   the Seventeenth Amendment

C   the Nineteenth Amendment

D   the Twenty-fourth Amendment

> "The right of citizens of the United States . . . shall not be
> denied or abridged in the United States or any State by reason
> of failure to pay any poll tax or other tax."
>
> —Twenty-fourth Amendment to the U.S. Constitution (1964)

16   As the above reading indicates, poll taxes were abolished in 1964. A poll tax is *best* described as

F   a tax on people with disabilities

G   a tax paid in order to vote

H   a tax that affects high-income groups more than low-income groups

J   a tax paid on one's property

17   **What caused the conflict known as the Whiskey Rebellion between Pennsylvania farmers and the national government?**

A   the passage of national Prohibition

B   the importation of cheap foreign whiskey to the United States

C   a federal ban on forming local militias

D   a federal tax on American-made whiskey

18   **Which of the following was *not* an attempt by northern and southern politicians to cooperate and settle the divisive issue of slavery?**

F   the Missouri Compromise

G   the American System

H   the Kansas-Nebraska Act

J   the Compromise of 1850

19   **The decades-long conflict between the United States and the Soviet Union was known as**

    A   the Vietnam War

    B   the Red Scare

    C   the Cold War

    D   the Cuban Missile Crisis

> "Full Faith and Credit shall be given in each State to the public Acts, Records, and judicial Proceedings of every other state."
>
> —Article IV, Section 1, of the U.S. Constitution

20   **Based on the above reading, which of the following statements is *most* correct?**

    F   States cannot have laws that conflict with laws of other states.

    G   States can ignore the laws of other states.

    H   States must respect the laws of other states.

    J   A majority of states can force a single state to change its laws.

Governance and Civics   United States History

---

21   **The First Amendment protects**

A   freedom of religion and voting rights

B   freedom of assembly and of the press

C   freedom of speech and from cruel and unusual punishment

D   freedom from unreasonable searches and seizures

22   **Which amendments describe the procedures that courts must use when trying people accused of crimes?**

F   the First, Second, and Third amendments

G   the Fourth and Fifth amendments

H   the Sixth, Seventh, and Eighth amendments

J   the Ninth and Tenth amendments

Governance and Civics   United States History

23   **The Bill of Rights consists of the rights listed**

    A   in the First Amendment to the Constitution

    B   in the preamble to the Constitution

    C   in all the amendments to the Constitution

    D   in the first 10 amendments to the Constitution

> "Nor shall any person be subject for the same offence to be twice put in jeopardy of life or limb . . ."
>
> —Fifth Amendment to the U.S. Constitution

24   **Based on the above reading, which of the following *best* describes the meaning of *double jeopardy*?**

    F   being tried twice for similar crimes

    G   being tried twice for the same crime

    H   being tried in both civil and criminal courts

    J   being tried in both state and federal courts

25   **Which of the following *best* describes the ruling in the Supreme Court case *Dred Scott* v. *Sandford*?**

     A   Slaves gained their freedom by living on free soil.

     B   Slaves had a constitutional right to buy their own freedom.

     C   The Missouri Compromise was constitutional.

     D   Slaves had no rights as U.S. citizens.

26   **The Supreme Court case *Marbury* v. *Madison* established the principle of judicial review. What is judicial review?**

     F   the power to examine the conduct of the President

     G   the right to hear cases rejected by lower courts

     H   the power to declare laws unconstitutional

     J   the authority to appoint new justices to the Supreme Court

Governance and Civics   United States History

27 **Which Supreme Court case established that federal laws take priority over state laws?**

A   *McCulloch* v. *Maryland*

B   *Worcester* v. *Georgia*

C   *Plessy* v. *Ferguson*

D   *Miranda* v. *Arizona*

28 **What was the effect of the *Brown* v. *Topeka Board of Education* decision by the Supreme Court?**

F   Jim Crow laws remained legal.

G   The separate-but-equal doctrine was declared unconstitutional.

H   Voting rights for African Americans were established.

J   Schools were banned from using racial quotas.

> "The most stringent protection of free speech would not protect a man in falsely shouting fire in a theatre and causing a panic."
>
> —Justice Oliver Wendell Holmes

29 **Based on the reading above, under which of the following situations might freedom of speech *not* be protected?**

A   A person loudly disagrees with the views of a politician.

B   A person insults another person in public.

C   A person on the corner shouts that the end of the world is coming.

D   A person tells a lie that endangers the safety of others.

---

30 **What might give a local government a reasonable cause to deny a parade permit to a group of marchers?**

F   The marchers are members of an unpopular minority group.

G   The march is religious in nature.

H   The march would block access to a hospital.

J   The marchers are members of a racist organization.

> **bail:** money or property an accused person gives a court to
> hold as a guarantee that he or she will appear for trial

31 **The Eighth Amendment states that "excessive bail shall not be required."
Why might this right be open to interpretation?**

A   The amendment applies only to cases tried in federal court.

B   People may disagree about what amount of bail counts as "excessive."

C   The judge can recommend a bail amount without requiring it.

D   Not all states ratified this particular amendment.

32 **When might a government prevent someone from practicing his or her
religion?**

F   never, because the government cannot interfere with freedom of religion

G   when the individual is a resident but not a U.S. citizen

H   when the local community does not like the person's religion

J   when the person's religious practices break other laws

> **annex:** to take control of land and make it part of a nation or state

33 **Which of the following individuals played a key role in the U.S. annexation of Texas?**

A   Sam Houston

B   Andrew Johnson

C   Henry Clay

D   Abraham Lincoln

34 **Who was the first person from west of the Appalachian Mountains elected president of the United States?**

F   James Monroe

G   Martin Van Buren

H   Andrew Jackson

J   Andrew Johnson

Governance and Civics   United States History

---

35   **During the presidency of James K. Polk, the United States gained a large amount of territory as a result of what event?**

     A   the purchase of Alaska from Russia

     B   American victory in the Mexican-American War

     C   California becoming a state

     D   Britain ceding the Oregon Territory to the United States

36   **The Cherokee leader Sequoyah is best known for what achievement?**

     F   He never lost a battle against the U.S. Army.

     G   He created a writing system for the Cherokee language.

     H   He was the first Native American elected to the U.S. Congress.

     J   He led explorers to the coast of California.

> **nomads:** people who move from place to place constantly in search of food sources

1 **Which Native American culture lived as nomads following the herds of buffalo?**

    A   the Native Americans of the Great Plains

    B   the Native Americans of the Arctic

    C   the Native Americans of the Southwest

    D   the Native Americans of the Northeast

2 **Which early American civilization built large road networks in the Andes Mountains?**

    F   the Mayan

    G   the Olmec

    H   the Aztec

    J   the Inca

3   The Mississippian culture is known for which of the following
     achievements?

     A   building large stone temples

     B   building great ceremonial mounds of earth

     C   building shelters of snow and ice called igloos

     D   building homes from adobe

> **hieroglyphic:** a system of writing that uses picture-like
> symbols called glyphs; different glyphs can represent words,
> sounds, or ideas

4   Which of the following early American civilizations created its own system
     of hieroglyphics?

     F   the Iroquois

     G   the Mayan

     H   the Inuit

     J   the Navajo

5   **What was the capital city of the Aztec Empire, with a population of some 400,000 people in 1519?**

   A   Machu Picchu

   B   Tenochtitlán

   C   Chaco

   D   El Dorado

6   **Members of the Native Americans in the Northwest carved and painted images of animals and spirits onto large logs known as**

   F   kachinas

   G   dreamcatchers

   H   totem poles

   J   kayaks

Voting Rights

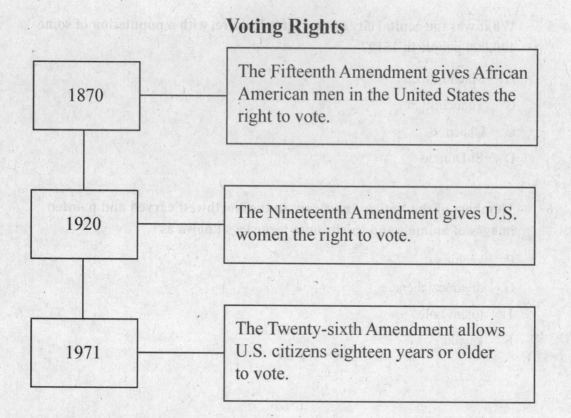

1870 — The Fifteenth Amendment gives African American men in the United States the right to vote.

1920 — The Nineteenth Amendment gives U.S. women the right to vote.

1971 — The Twenty-sixth Amendment allows U.S. citizens eighteen years or older to vote.

7   **Based on the time line shown above, which of the following people would have had the legal right to vote anywhere in the United States in 1900?**

   A   an 18 year-old white man

   B   a 60 year-old white woman

   C   a 40 year-old African American man

   D   a 20 year-old African American woman

8   **About how many years passed between the ratification of each of the amendments shown above?**

   F   about 100 years

   G   about 50 years

   H   about 25 years

   J   about 10 years

History

United States History

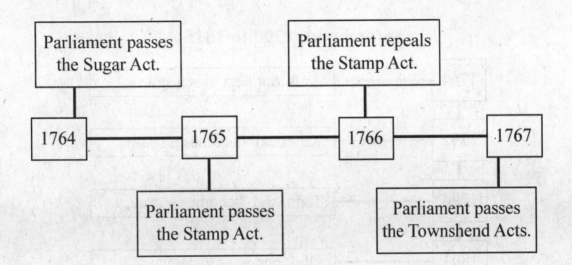

9   **Use the time line shown above to place the acts passed by Parliament in order from first to last.**

    A   Sugar Act, Townshend Act, Stamp Act

    B   Sugar Act, Stamp Act, Townshend Act

    C   Stamp Act, Townshend Act, Sugar Act

    D   Townshend Act, Stamp Act, Sugar Act

10 **Based on the time line shown above, how many acts did Parliament pass between 1765 and 1767?**

    F   one

    G   two

    H   three

    J   four

Statehood, 1790 to 1815

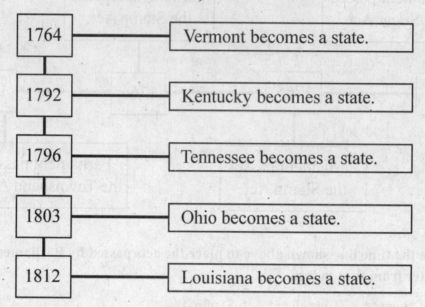

1764	Vermont becomes a state.
1792	Kentucky becomes a state.
1796	Tennessee becomes a state.
1803	Ohio becomes a state.
1812	Louisiana becomes a state.

11 Put the following states in the order that they joined the Union, from first to last: Ohio, Vermont, and Tennessee.

A   Vermont, Ohio, Tennessee

B   Ohio, Tennessee, Vermont

C   Vermont, Tennessee, Ohio

D   Tennessee, Vermont, Ohio

12 What is the greatest length of time shown on the time line above between the admission of states to the Union?

F   3 years

G   5 years

H   9 years

J   10 years

13 **A primary source is**

    A   a source that is more important than other sources

    B   the first source listed in a bibliography

    C   a firsthand source of historical information

    D   the source referred to most often in a book

14 **A description of an event written after the event took place by someone who did not take part in or witness that event is known as**

    F   a primary source

    G   a secondary source

    H   a natural source

    J   an artificial source

List of Sources A

a written speech

a letter written by a person who watched the speech

a recording of the person giving the speech

a biography of the person who wrote the speech

15   **Which of the sources listed above is *not* a primary source?**

A   the speech

B   the letter

C   the recording

D   the biography

List of Sources B

an encyclopedia

an editorial cartoon

a newspaper report

a history textbook

16   **Which pair of sources listed above are secondary sources?**

F   the encyclopedia and editorial cartoon

G   the editorial cartoon and newspaper report

H   the newspaper report and the history textbook

J   the encyclopedia and the history textbook

> **autobiography:** a history of a person's life written by that
> person

17   **Based on the definition given above, an autobiography is**

A   a primary source

B   a secondary source

C   neither a primary nor a secondary source

D   both a primary and a secondary source

---

18   **Which are more reliable, primary sources or secondary sources?**

F   Primary sources are more reliable.

G   Secondary sources are more reliable.

H   No type of source is always more reliable than another.

J   All sources are equally reliable.

19 The migration of English colonists to the western frontier was a major cause of

A   a decline in the size of American cities

B   conflict with Native Americans

C   improved relations with Britain

D   epidemics that spread back to the East

20 How did the French and Indian War contribute to the start of the Revolutionary War?

F   Britain placed the colonies under military rule during the war.

G   Colonists were angry because the war stopped westward expansion.

H   Parliament raised taxes on the colonies to help pay the cost of the war.

J   Colonists began to ally with the victorious French.

21 **To create a government uniting all the colonies during the American Revolution, colonists ratified the document known as**

   A   the Declaration of Independence

   B   the Articles of Confederation

   C   the Constitution

   D   the Northwest Ordinance

---

embargo: banning trade with another country

impressment: the practice of forcing people, including foreign citizens, to serve in the army or navy against their will

---

22 **Which of the following events was *not* a cause of the War of 1812?**

   F   a British embargo on trade with the United States

   G   a U.S. embargo on trade with Great Britain

   H   the impressment of American sailors by the British navy

   J   the impressment of British sailors by the American navy

23 **As a result of the War of 1812**

A   the United States gained the Oregon Territory

B   Great Britain gained part of the state of Maine

C   the Indian Territory was created

D   neither side gained any territory

Parliament: the national legislative body of Great Britain

24 **One of the key causes of the American Revolution was the debate between the colonies and Parliament over**

F   taxation without representation

G   the printing of colonial money

H   the British ban on the slave trade

J   the draft of colonial citizens into the British army

25 The Mexican-American War was caused in large part by a dispute over the annexation of

A   California

B   New Mexico

C   Texas

D   Cuba

26 What name was given to the path taken by the Cherokees forced to move to the Indian Territory?

F   the Long Walk

G   the Trail of Tears

H   the Indian Trail

J   the Overland Trail

The Missouri Compromise

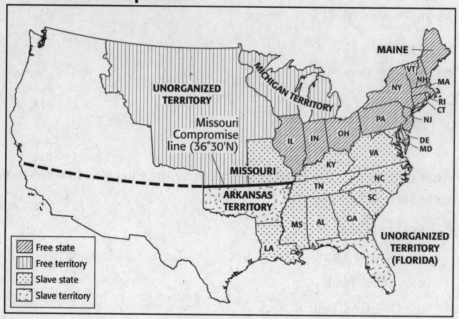

27 **Based on the information in the map above, what major issue divided the United States as it expanded to the West?**

A what to name the unorganized territories

B how many states could be admitted into the Union

C whether new states would allow slavery

D how many representatives each new state would have

28 **What was the purpose of the 36° 30' N line shown on the map?**

F New states south of the line would be admitted as slave states.

G New states south of the line would be admitted as free states.

H No new states would be admitted south of the line.

J No new states would be admitted north of the line.

29 **Based on the information in the map on the facing page, how many free and slave states were there when the Missouri Compromise was made?**

   A   10 free states and 10 slave states

   B   12 free states and 12 slave states

   C   12 free states and 10 slave states

   D   13 slave states and 11 free states

30 **The Gold Rush of 1849 led to the rapid settlement and statehood of**

   F   New Mexico

   G   Colorado

   H   California

   J   Nevada

31   **The Lewis and Clark Expedition was made possible by which of the following?**

A   the Proclamation of 1763

B   the invention of the steamboat

C   the Louisiana Purchase

D   the Oregon Trail

32   **Why did the majority of early pioneers heading to the West settle near the Pacific coast?**

F   The land and climate closer to the Pacific coast were better for farming.

G   powerful Native Americans controlled the Southwest.

H   The pioneers could not grow crops on the Great Plains.

J   The pioneers preferred to live under Spanish rule.

> **Northwest Passage:** a long-rumored sea route to Asia cutting through the North American continent

33 **Which of the following were reasons why Europeans explored the Americas?**

A   They were searching for the Northwest Passage.

B   They hoped to find spices and silks.

C   They hoped to spread Christianity to new peoples.

D   All of the above.

34 **Which of the following was *not* a cause of conflict between the North and South?**

F   the northern factories' boycott of southern cotton

G   the Fugitive Slave Act

H   the publication of *Uncle Tom's Cabin*

J   the northern abolitionist movement

35 **Which of the following events increased tensions between the North and South leading up to the Civil War?**

A   the assassination of James Garfield

B   John Brown's Raid

C   the Bear Flag Revolt

D   the Seneca Falls Convention

> **transcontinental:** reaching from one end of a continent to the other

36 **Why was the transcontinental railroad built?**

F   to carry Union troops to the western theater of battle

G   to divide the United States along the 36° 30' N line

H   to open the West to further settlement and development

J   to reach the gold fields of California

> **conquistadores:** Spanish soldiers and explorers who led
> expeditions in the Americas

---

37 **The Aztec Empire was conquered by the conquistador known as**

    A   Ponce de León

    B   Pizarro

    C   Coronado

    D   Cortés

---

38 **Which of the following *best* describes what happened to Native American populations after the arrival of Europeans?**

    F   Large numbers of Native Americans immigrated to Europe.

    G   The Native American population increased as new crops were introduced.

    H   The Native American population fell drastically.

    J   The Native American population remained stable.

39 **Which of the following factors caused the greatest number of deaths among Native Americans after Europeans arrived?**

A   warfare with European colonists

B   warfare among Native American cultures

C   starvation due to massive crop failures

D   diseases introduced by Europeans to the Americas

---

extinction: the act of eliminating all members of an animal or plant species

40 **European settlers drove which of the following animal species into extinction?**

F   bison

G   wolves

H   passenger pigeons

J   mountain lions

41 Much of what is now Canada was originally part of which European colony?

A   New England

B   New France

C   New Spain

D   New Netherlands

---

technology: the use of knowledge in a practical way to achieve certain results, such as building machinery

---

42 Which of the following technologies was *not* introduced to North America by European settlers?

F   gunpowder

G   weaving

H   iron tools

J   clocks

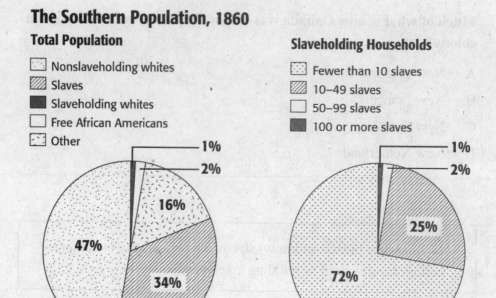

The Southern Population, 1860

Total Population

- ▫ Nonslaveholding whites
- ▨ Slaves
- ■ Slaveholding whites
- ☐ Free African Americans
- ⬚ Other

Slaveholding Households

- ▫ Fewer than 10 slaves
- ▨ 10–49 slaves
- ☐ 50–99 slaves
- ■ 100 or more slaves

Total Population pie chart: 1%, 2%, 16%, 47%, 34%

Slaveholding Households pie chart: 1%, 2%, 25%, 72%

Sources: Historical Statistics of the United States; The Black American Reference Book; Slavery and the Southern Economy

43 **What were the two largest population groups in the South in 1860?**

A   white slaveholders and slaves

B   white slaveholders and white nonslaveholders

C   slaves and white nonslaveholders

D   slaves and free African Americans

44 **What percentage of southern slaveholders had more than 100 slaves?**

F   72

G   25

H   2

J   1

United States History

45 **Who were the wealthiest and most influential members of southern society?**

A   white slaveholders with many slaves

B   white slaveholders with a few slaves

C   white farmers who owned no slaves

D   white factory owners who owned no slaves

46 **The majority of southern slaves did what type of labor?**

F   They worked as domestic servants in southern homes.

G   They grew cash crops such as cotton, rice, and sugar.

H   They mined minerals such as coal and iron.

J   They worked as craftspeople building fine goods.

Free and Slave States

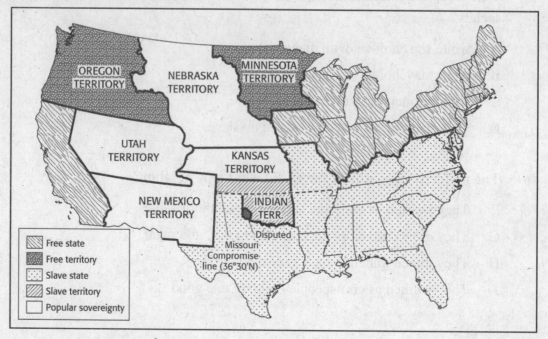

47 Based on the map above, which of the following *best* describes the balance of slave and free states at the time shown on the map?

A There were more slave states than free states.

B There were more free states than slave states.

C There were an equal number of free and slave states.

D There were more slave territories than free territories.

48 What did southern politicians fear would happen if no new slave states were admitted to the United States?

F Demand for southern cotton would decrease.

G Southern slave states would lose influence in the U.S. Congress.

H The slave trade with Mexico would have to be abandoned.

J Trade with Canada would decline.

New Political Parties

1839	The Liberty Party is founded to oppose the spread of slavery
1848	The Free Soil Party is formed and calls for "Free Soil, Free Speech, Free Labor, and Free Men."
1854	The Republican Party is formed by antislavery and reform groups.
1860	The Constitutional Union Party is formed to uphold "the Constitution of the Country, the Union of the States, and the enforcement of the laws."

49   What common idea was shared by most of the parties shown in the time line above?

   A   They opposed westward expansion and development.

   B   They wanted higher tariffs.

   C   They opposed the expansion of slavery.

   D   They demanded religious reform.

50   Based on the information in the time line above, which of the following statements is correct?

   F   The Liberty Party was created by former Republicans.

   G   The Free Soil Party was formed 5 years before the Republican Party.

   H   The Republican Party was founded 15 years after the Liberty Party.

   J   Most of these parties were formed in the 1840s.

Political Party Breakups

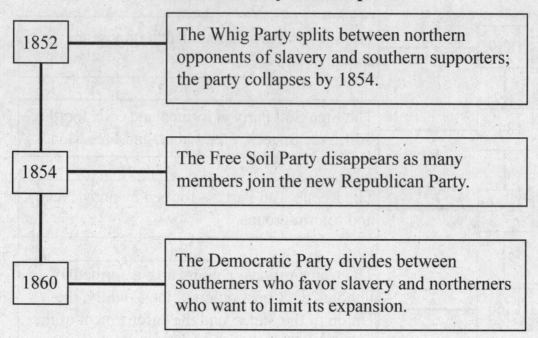

1852 — The Whig Party splits between northern opponents of slavery and southern supporters; the party collapses by 1854.

1854 — The Free Soil Party disappears as many members join the new Republican Party.

1860 — The Democratic Party divides between southerners who favor slavery and northerners who want to limit its expansion.

51 Which of the following statements *best* describes what happened in 1854 to the political parties shown in the time line above?

    A   The Free Soil Party ceased to exist.

    B   The Whig Party ceased to exist.

    C   The Free Soil and Whig Parties ceased to exist.

    D   The Free Soil Party members joined the Whigs.

52 Based on the information in the time line above, what role did the issue of slavery play in the breakup of political parties?

    F   Slavery played no significant role.

    G   Slavery divided parties along northern and southern lines.

    H   Slavery divided parties along eastern and western lines.

    J   Slavery divided political parties within the South.

The 1860 Presidential Election

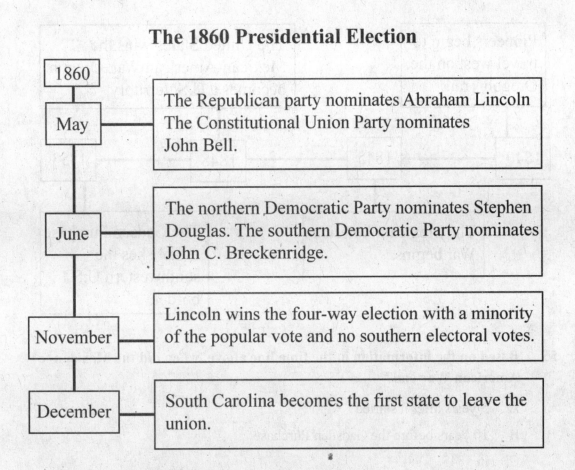

1860

May — The Republican party nominates Abraham Lincoln The Constitutional Union Party nominates John Bell.

June — The northern Democratic Party nominates Stephen Douglas. The southern Democratic Party nominates John C. Breckenridge.

November — Lincoln wins the four-way election with a minority of the popular vote and no southern electoral votes.

December — South Carolina becomes the first state to leave the union.

53 **Which of the following events helped Lincoln win the presidency?**

A   He received no southern electoral votes.

B   The Democratic Party split its vote between two candidates.

C   He won a clear majority of the popular vote.

D   Seminole in the South

54 **Why was South Carolina's leaving the Union important?**

F   It was the first step toward the forming of the Confederacy.

G   South Carolina was Lincoln's home state.

H   It caused a recount of the electoral votes.

J   South Carolina was the only source of cotton for the nation.

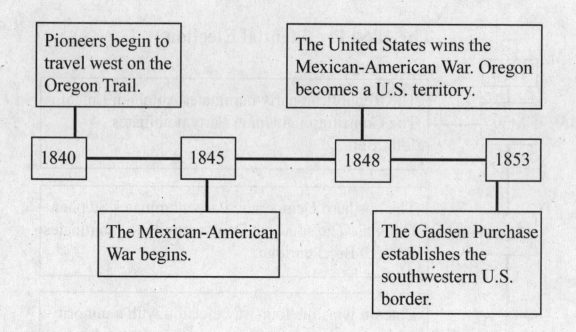

55 **Based on the information in the time line above, when did the Mexican-American War end?**

A   5 years after it started

B   10 years before the Gadsden Purchase

C   in 1845

D   in the same year that Oregon became a U.S. territory

56 **Based on the information in the time line above, which of the following statements is *false*?**

F   The Gadsden Purchase took place in 1853.

G   The U.S. victory in the Mexican-American War allowed pioneers to go to Oregon.

H   The Mexican-American War did not set the southwestern border of the United States.

J   Oregon became a territory three years after the Mexican-American War started.

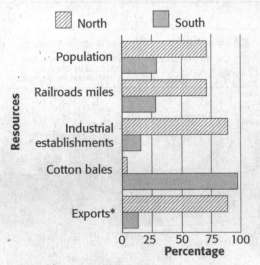

Resources of the North and South

North   South

*Southern exports do not include Tennessee, Arkansas, and Mississippi

---

57 How would you describe the population of the United States based on the information in the graph above?

A   The North had a population of nearly 75 million.

B   The North had five times the population of the South.

C   About one in every four Americans lived in the South.

D   The South had just under 20 percent of the nation's population.

58 Based on the information shown in the graph above, which of the following statements is *most* correct?

F   The North led the South in every category shown on the graph.

G   The southern economy was less industrial than the northern economy.

H   The South accounted for most of the nation's exports.

J   The North had 10 times the railroad miles of the South.

Emancipation Proclamation

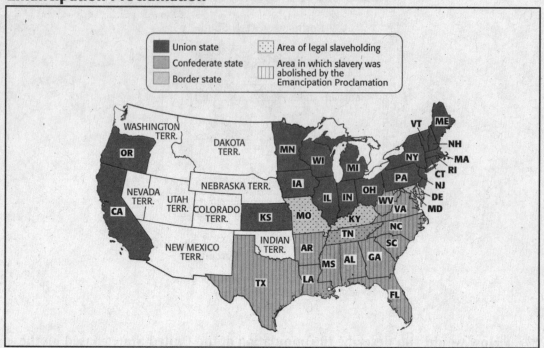

59 **Based on the information shown in the map, what did the Emancipation Proclamation do?**

A   abolished slavery in the Union states

B   abolished slavery in nearly all the border states

C   abolished slavery in the Confederate states

D   abolished slavery in almost all the Confederate states

60 **In which pair of the following regions was slavery still legal after the Emancipation Proclamation?**

F   Missouri and Tennessee

G   West Virginia and Maryland

H   Kentucky and the Indian Territory

J   Arkansas and Delaware

> "The laws of the United States must be executed. I have no discretionary power on the subject—my duty is emphatically pronounced in the Constitution . . . Disunion, by armed force, is TREASON. Are you ready to incur its guilt? If you are, on the head of the instigators of the act be the dreadful consequences . . . Fellow-citizens of the United States! . . . I rely with equal confidence on your undivided support in my determination to execute the laws—to preserve the Union by all constitutional means."
>
> —Andrew Jackson speaking to Congress about the Nullification Crisis

61 **During the Nullification Crisis, South Carolina threatened to leave the Union because**

A it disagreed with the "necessary and proper" clause of the Constitution

B it opposed the law chartering the Bank of the United States

C it would not support the Tariff of 1832

D the U.S. government tried to abolish slavery in South Carolina

62 **Based on the reading above, what was President Andrew Jackson's view of the Nullification Crisis?**

F Any state had the right to leave the Union if it wished.

G Congress would have to vote whether to allow South Carolina to leave.

H Congress should make the changes requested by South Carolina.

J No state had a right to defy federal laws or leave the Union.

"'A house divided against itself cannot stand.' I believe this government cannot endure, permanently, half slave and half free. I do not expect the Union to be dissolved; I do not expect the house to fall; but I do expect it will cease to be divided. It will become all one thing, or all the other."

—Abraham Lincoln, 1858

63 **Based on the reading above, what does Lincoln believe will happen to the United States as a result of slavery?**

A   The nation will remain split between free and slave states.

B   The nation will split into two completely different countries.

C   Slavery will become legal in every state or be banned in every state.

D   No new states will join the Union.

64 **Which *best* explains why the quotation above is a primary source?**

F   Anything written by a president is a primary source.

G   It tells Lincoln's personal views on history as it took place.

H   It discusses important political events.

J   It was written by a single person.

The Battle of Gettysburg

Confederate general Robert E. Lee hoped that his invasion of the North would strike a major blow against the enemy. A victory on northern soil in 1863 might even encourage neutral European nations to ally with the Confederate cause. However, Lee's defeat at the Battle of Gettysburg was a serious setback for the Confederacy. Both sides suffered terrible losses in the bloodiest battle of the Civil War. Lee was never again able to invade the northern states. The hoped-for European support never came. The Battle of Gettysburg was thus a turning point in the war in favor of the Union.

65 **According to this secondary source, what was the importance of the Battle of Gettysburg?**

A   It was a key victory for the Confederacy.

B   It was a key victory for the Union.

C   It crippled both armies.

D   It ended the war in a stalemate.

66 **Which of the following conclusions *cannot* be drawn from the information presented in this source?**

F   The Battle of Gettysburg won the war for the Union.

G   A Confederate victory at Gettysburg would have won the war for the South.

H   European nations would never have allied with the Confederacy.

J   Many more Confederate troops than Union troops died in the battle.

> "The property and sovereignty of all Louisiana . . . have on certain conditions been transferred to the United States by instruments bearing date the 30th of April last. While the property and sovereignty of the Mississippi and its waters secure an independent outlet for the produce of the western States, and an uncontrolled navigation through their whole course . . . the fertility of the country, its climate and extent, promise in due season important aids to our treasury, an ample provision for our posterity, and a wide-spread field for the blessings of freedom and equal laws."
>
> —Thomas Jefferson

67 **What is one clue provided by the reading above that it is a primary source document?**

A It describes the Louisiana Purchase.

B It gives a positive account of the Louisiana Territory.

C It identifies the purchase as having taken place recently.

D It refers to the Mississippi River as an important waterway.

68 **Which of the following is *not* a reason given by Jefferson for supporting the Louisiana Purchase?**

F It will secure access to the Mississippi River.

G It will provide valuable resources for the United States.

H It will protect the western states from attack by Native Americans.

J It will promote the spread of liberty and democracy.

> "The people of the young Republic of the United States were greatly astonished, in the summer of 1803, to learn that Napoleon Bonaparte, then First Consul of France, had sold to us the vast tract of land known as the country of Louisiana . . . The scheme was ridiculed by persons who insisted that the region was not only wild and unexplored, but uninhabitable and worthless . . . In addition to its being a foolish bargain, it was urged that President Jefferson had no right, under the constitution of the United States, to add any territory to the area of the Republic . . . Nevertheless, a majority of the people were in favor of the purchase . . . This momentous transfer took place one hundred years ago."
>
> —from *First Across the Continent,* Noah Brooks

69 **What is one clue provided by the reading above that it is a secondary source document?**

A   It was not written by Thomas Jefferson.

B   It includes criticism of the Louisiana Purchase.

C   It refers to the Louisiana Purchase as having been made many years ago.

D   It mentions Napoleon Bonaparte.

70 **According to the passage above, why were some people critical of the Louisiana Purchase?**

F   They wanted to conquer the Louisiana Territory, not buy it.

G   They thought the land was worthless.

H   They wanted Jefferson to buy more land than he did.

J   They wanted to buy Mexico from Spain.

71 **Which of the following is a primary source document?**

   A   a historical marker on the Lewis and Clark Trail

   B   a page from Clark's journal

   C   a magazine article about the Lewis and Clark Expedition

   D   a documentary film about the Lewis and Clark Expedition

72 **Identify one advantage secondary source documents can have over primary source documents.**

   F   firsthand information on historical events

   G   greater value as a historical artifact

   H   a broader perspective on events of the past

   J   knowledge of what individual people were thinking

Indian Removal from the Southeast, 1830s

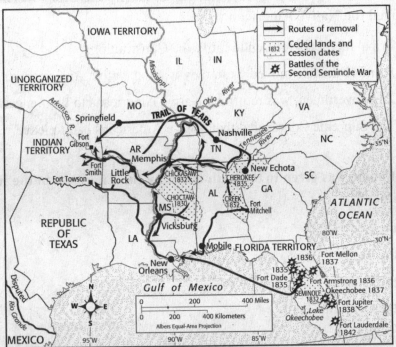

73 **Based on the map shown above, what happened to the major Native American groups of the Southeast?**

A   They settled in Florida.

B   They settled in the lands marked on the map as ceded lands.

C   They were forced to move west of the Mississippi River.

D   They became citizens of the southern states where they lived.

74 **What Native American group shown on the map fought U.S. troops in Florida?**

F   the Creeks

G   the Cherokees

H   the Chickasaws

J   the Seminoles

75   Which of the following factors *best* explains why the U.S. government
     removed the Native American tribes?

    A   Tribal members refused to ratify the Constitution.

    B   As more settlers moved west, they wanted Native American lands.

    C   The government was returning Native Americans to their ancestral homes.

    D   The Supreme Court ruled that Native Americans had to leave.

76   What name was given to the path taken by the Cherokee to the Indian
     Territory?

    F   the Long Walk

    G   the Trail of Tears

    H   the Indian Trail

    J   the Overland Trail

Battle of Saratoga

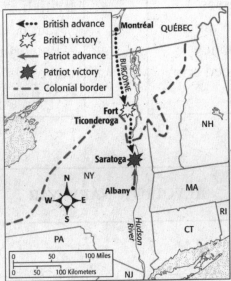

77   **The Battle of Saratoga was fought in what state?**

A   New York

B   New Hampshire

C   Pennsylvania

D   Québec

78   **The Patriot victory at Saratoga stopped the British from reaching what destination?**

F   Fort Ticonderoga

G   the Hudson River

H   Albany

J   Massachusetts

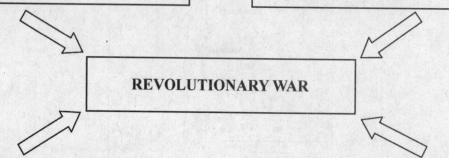

American Weaknesses
- Weak central government
- Trouble raising money
- Small, inexperienced army
- Weak navy

British Strengths
- Large, experienced army
- Powerful navy
- Wealthy economy
- Native American allies

REVOLUTIONARY WAR

American Strengths
- Fighting on home soil
- Could fight a guerrilla war
- Leadership of Washington
- Determination to win

British Weaknesses
- Fighting on unfamiliar ground
- Long lines of supply and communication

79   Using the diagram above, identify two military strengths of the Americans.

    A   They fought on familiar ground and had an experienced army.

    B   They had good leadership and a strong will to win.

    C   They had a powerful navy and a rich economy.

    D   They had a strong central government and could fight a guerrilla war.

80   Based on the diagram above, what was the *biggest* disadvantage faced by the British?

    F   They could not afford to pay for the war.

    G   Their army had little battle experience.

    H   They were fighting far from their homeland.

    J   Most Native Americans sided with the Patriots.

81 Based on the information given in the diagram on the facing page, what type of conflict would favor the American forces?

  A   a short war in which they could use their superior numbers

  B   a long war in which they could slowly wear down the British

  C   a naval war in which they could fight mainly at sea

  D   an American invasion of Britain

82 Which of the following factors helped General Washington win the decisive victory at Yorktown that ended the war?

  F   The Hessian soldiers hired by the British joined the Americans.

  G   Superior American cannons broke the British defenses.

  H   The French army and navy aided the American forces.

  J   Cornwallis mistakenly thought he was outnumbered and gave up.

Paul Revere's Ride

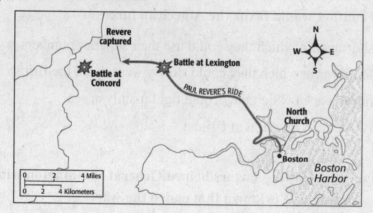

1 **What did Paul Revere accomplish with his famous ride?**

A   He warned the Minutemen in time for them to escape.

B   His warning prepared the Minutemen for the Battle of Lexington.

C   His warning allowed the Continental Congress to flee to safety.

D   He reached Concord in time to lead the Patriot troops there.

---

2 **How did Thomas Paine influence the American Revolution?**

F   by calling for independence from Britain in his pamphlet *Common Sense*

G   by advising General Washington on military strategy

H   by helping write the Declaration of Independence

J   by serving the Patriots as a spy in Great Britain

Individuals, Groups, and Interactions United States History

3 Which group of Native Americans founded a democratic confederacy?

    A   the Navajos

    B   the Aztecs

    C   the Iroquois

    D   the Pueblos

4 The War Hawks, who included politician Henry Clay, were members of the U.S. Congress who supported a war against

    F   Mexico

    G   France

    H   Great Britain

    J   Spain

5 **The Federalists**

   A   supported ratification of the U.S. Constitution

   B   opposed ratification of the U.S. Constitution

   C   supported the Loyalist cause during the Revolution

   D   supported secession from the Union

6 **What did the representatives of small states and large states achieve at the Constitutional Convention by agreeing to the Great Compromise?**

   F   They abolished slavery in the United States.

   G   They divided the federal government into three branches.

   H   They established a Congress with two houses.

   J   They agreed to count three-fifths of slaves as part of the population for taxation purposes.

Individuals, Groups, and Interactions United States History

7 **Which of the following groups played the greatest role in ending the transatlantic slave trade between Africa and the United States?**

A   the Whigs

B   the Tories

C   the abolitionists

D   factory owners

---

suffrage: the right to vote

8 **At what meeting did supporters of women's suffrage gather to launch a movement for women's rights in America?**

F   the Constitutional Convention

G   the Seneca Falls Convention

H   the Convention of 1818

J   Walden Pond

The Underground Railroad

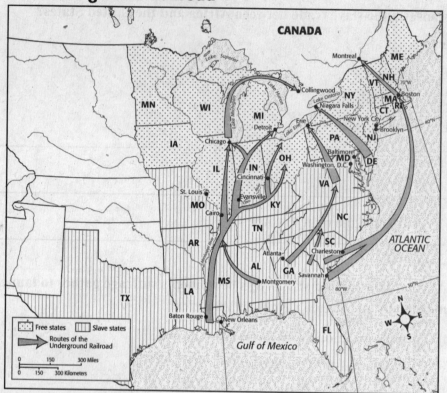

9 **Why did African Americans flee the South using the so-called Underground Railroad?**

A Free African Americans had few rights in most of the South.

B Enslaved African families were split up at slave auctions.

C African American slaves were often cruelly punished by their slaveholders.

D All of the above

10 **Which of the following groups promoted negative stereotypes of foreign immigrants in the United States?**

F nativists

G carpetbaggers

H sodbusters

J freedmen

> **altruism:** unselfish acts that benefit those other than yourself

---

11 **Based on the definition given above, which of the following groups _best_ demonstrated altruism in their actions?**

    A   colonists who dumped tea into Boston Harbor

    B   bounty hunters paid to capture fugitive slaves

    C   forty-niners seeking gold in California

    D   white northerners helping slaves escape on the Underground Railroad

---

> **conformity:** acting in the same way as others according to the customs or views of the majority

---

12 **Which of the following individuals left the Massachusetts Bay Colony to protest the religious conformity demanded by its leaders?**

    F   Sojourner Truth

    G   Roger Williams

    H   Cotton Mather

    J   George Whitfield

> **revivals:** public church meetings in which ministers preach to large audiences, often in an emotional style

13 **Which of the following events inspired many revivals and helped create new reform movements?**

  A   the Half-Way Covenant

  B   the Mayflower Compact

  C   the Second Great Awakening

  D   the XYZ Affair

14 **Supporters of which reform movement were *best* known for trying to limit the consumption of alcohol by American families?**

  F   abolitionist movement

  G   temperance movement

  H   suffrage movement

  J   common-school movement

Individuals, Groups, and Interactions   United States History

15 **Which of the following did the Civil Rights Act passed by Congress in 1964 accomplish?**

A   It upheld the Supreme Court ruling in *Plessy* v. *Ferguson.*

B   It declared racial discrimination in employment or voting to be illegal.

C   It passed a series of regulations known as Jim Crow laws.

D   It made hate crimes federal offenses.

16 **Gallaudet University was founded in the 1860s to educate which group of Americans?**

F   the hearing impaired

G   the visually impaired

H   women

J   African Americans

17 Which of the following national organizations works with teachers, parents, schools, and federal agencies to improve public education?

   A   ACT

   B   SAT

   C   TPA

   D   PTA

18 Which of the following nongovernmental groups is authorized by Congress to assist federal agencies with disaster relief?

   F   Blue Shield

   G   Red Cross

   H   FEMA

   J   NATO

Individuals, Groups, and Interactions United States History

19 **In what way do private groups work with local governments to help meet the needs of local communities?**

A   by setting up neighborhood watch groups to fight crime

B   by opening food banks for the hungry

C   by establishing and operating homeless shelters

D   all of the above

20 **Local governments rely most commonly on volunteers to assist with which important public service?**

F.   serving on juries during criminal cases

G   running local polling stations during elections

H   repairing major public roads and buildings

J   collecting taxes

Civics Scenario

The city government owns a few empty lots located near a neighborhood and a few blocks from a school. The city council is trying to decide whether to sell the land to a developer who will build stores there or to turn the land into a park.

21 **Should the city council explain its plans to the public and ask for their input? Choose the answer that *best* reflects democratic ideals.**

A   no, because the city council has the authority to do whatever it wants

B   no, because citizens might disagree about which plan they support

C   yes, because either proposed plan will affect nearby homes and the school

D   yes, because city councils should not make any decisions without asking the public

22 **How might the city council get input from citizens on the proposed plans for the empty lots?**

F   make the plans ballot initiatives that citizens could vote on at the next local election

G   hold public meetings for citizens to voice their views before the city council

H   conduct an opinion survey of business and home owners in the neighborhood

J   all of the above

Individuals, Groups, and Interactions   United States History

23   **Which of the following historical periods was *most* noted for the many social reform movements begun by citizens and public officials?**

    A   the Progressive Era

    B   the Roaring Twenties

    C   the Gilded Age

    D   the Gold Rush

24   **Which of the following methods is used by citizens in some states to propose their own laws to the state legislature?**

    F   referendum

    G   initiative

    H   recall

    J   extradition